Spoken Words from My Heart
Book of Poems

Email: dedrawaller@gmail.com

Facebook: www.facebook.com/iamdedra.com

Copyright © 2012, 2021 by Dedra Shanell Haynes-Waller

All rights reserved solely by the author. No part of this book may be reproduced, stored in a retrieval system, or transmitted in any form or by any means without expressed written permission of the author.

All content was provided to the publisher as original author work, not infringing on the copyrights of others.

Effective Date of Registration: September 25, 2012

ISBN: 978-1-62407-217-8
Printed in the U.S.A.

Spoken Words From My eart

Book of Poems

Dedra Haynes-Waller

Table of Contents

Acknowledgments	1
Introduction	2
This is for real isn't it?	3
The Day I Fell In Love	4
I Will Always Care About You	5
Still Loving You	6
LOST	7
What Happened?	8
Grace	9
Lord, I Need Your Understanding	10
Where, am I and what do I do?	11
Forever In My Heart?	12
He Kept Me	13
Time is Ticking	14
What's Going On?	15
Here for the Changes	16
There's Been a Change in My Life	17
Changes	18
Is it a game or what?	19
Mothers Aren't so Bad	20
New Life	21
MANTLE	22
You Make Me Smile	23
ROSES	24
Where am I now?	25
We Are Who We Are	26
Closer or Not	27
Two Knock Outs	28
FATHERS	29
Tell Me How Many Times	30

Table of Contents

Today & Tomorrow	31
Where's the truth?	32
Am I worthy?	33
Happy Birthday	34
What a Time, Shock, in Life	35
Running, trying not to leave what God has for me!	36
There's a Shift Going On	37
Do you think I don't know?	38
Don't Let Your Life Lead You - You Might Want to Lead It!	39
Dear God	40
Do you really know?	41
CHANGE	42
Color Tells It!	43
HOME	44
NON-SENSE	45
Slowly Going Away	46
If I...	47
How can you love and hate at the same time?	48
It Comes Back!	49
UNIQUE	50
Praying Hands	51
Don't Give Up - Try Me, & See!	52
It is Well	53
God's Special Touch	54
About the Author	55

Acknowledgements

First and foremost, I want to acknowledge the one and only true and living God-Father, Son, and Holy Ghost-for giving me this gift so that I may be able to share it with many.

I am grateful for my husband, Darryl, for being there for me in so many ways. For the encouragement and the listening ear!

Also, to my daughter and son; DaShana & Ra'Keem for lending their helping hands and ears!

To Zanetta Collins, for such encouraging words, hands on works, help, and prayers!

I also say to Janice Carmicheal, thank you for your editing eyes and kind words of encouragement.

Most of all I thank my father and mother, George and Francine Haynes, for giving me life. Thank you so much!

Dedra Haynes-Waller

Introduction

These words I give to you as a token and piece of my soul. Through many hard trials and many lonely places, I found comfort in writing. Taking those not so good days and allowing God to bring about a change in my life.

And then there were those bittersweet days, that at one moment things seemed to be going right and then at the drop of a dime the mood shifted and caused time to display a bitter taste. Yet there were the good ol' days that the devil in hell could not change, they were right on the money!

Peace, joy, and happiness that would fill a crowded room and it mattered not who was in it - the rich, poor, strong, or the weak. Those were the days that I know God created just for me!

So as you begin to read and indulge in these words from my heart know that words can comfort, deliver and

Set You Free!

This is for real, isn't it?

For one minute don't you think our love is a game!

If you didn't know,
it doesn't feel close to any other or the same

The light shining so bright from the sun,
yet glistening in the night

When we started this love thing,
it got off quite ok and now it seems so right

You are to me now, like no other sweet love
As time goes on I thank the good Lord up above
Just imagine sitting with your lover, a dream forever

Holding on to someone
who can spend countless times whenever

I sometimes think of that grand ol' day
When we're exchanging vows and are happy in every way
Is this real or what?

The beautiful colors and flowers all different sorts of things
The lovely people and the joy our love brings
You, standing at the altar waiting for me to be hand and hand
Only to be together for a lifetime together we'll stand
Is this real love or what?

(1990)

Dedra Haynes-Waller

The Day I Fell In Love

The day I fell in love was the day I met you
I finally found the man that'd make my dreams come true
I almost couldn't believe the way my heart was glad
To know you're the best friend that I ever had
I can't make it without you and that's the way I feel
I know it's not a dream, because it's much too real

Maybe I'm pushing it and taken it too fast
But as long as I believe in it, I know it will last
You are my breath of life; you are my dream come true
And the day I fell in love was the day I met you
When I was down and out, feeling rather low
You showed me through the storms, the only friend I know

When no one else listens, you lend me your ear
When I thought I was all alone, you were standing right there
When I wanted to give up and turn back around
You told me you'd be there for me and you'll never let me down
When people laugh at my mistakes you help me make it through
I guess that's why I'm so in love with you.

(1990)

I Will Always Care About You

I sometimes think you really don't know
How very important you are to me,
You have put new meaning and awareness
When I think of how life really is to be.

I know closeness when we are together
I really care about you,
It's important to me that you are safe
And that you are well too
I feel a sense of loss when we're apart
Sometimes I wonder if it was love from the start.

Having more time together
Then I think about the comfort we share
Of your arms around me
That keeps me going for a while knowing your there
I know that soon we'll be together
Your touch will make all things better
In my world it always does you see
Wherever our decisions may take us
Hopefully you'll come back to me
I will always care about you
I will always remember what you do
There will always be a place for you in my heart
I will always care about you whenever we're apart.

(10/12/1990)

Dedra Haynes-Waller

Still Loving You

At one time we were friends, our loved slipped up so quickly
The laughs the cries and then a touch that seemed so endlessly
Right now I don't know where I stand
All I ask for is you meet me halfway and just lend your hand
I know there's someone else in your life right now, and that I can't change
But it's just whenever you're around, a part of me feels strange
I really love you deep down inside
The kind of love that's too deep to hide
When we were in love I knew something was wrong
Maybe if jealousy was left out, maybe we could sing a sweet song
It's hard for me to let go so easily
You were my first love and my feelings don't fade so quickly
If only I could turn back the times when we could laugh and play
Maybe you could think of me in a different way, not as we lay
I don't know what you did to me to make me feel this way
I just love you more than you'll ever know and more that I can say
Since neither of us can change the way we feel
I'll take it one day at a time as I allow my heart to heal
Hope we can be friends hope we can spend a little time
Don't act a fool as if it was a crime
Sorry there's a part of me that won't let go
I'm not saying this for fashion only to let you know
Remember the walks in the fancy mall
The plant that fell while we played in the hall
Remember the night of B B concert
Well I try to remember how you once felt and I still hurt
You were someone, anyone could love and appreciate
True, we both did wrong here and there, a little give and take,
that thin line of love and hate
Just as long as we keep in touch
Our love will never die, but will be just as much
If there's a place in your heat that's not taken or filled
Leave a place for me because mine still isn't healed
I must say we tried but it just didn't work
So let's be friends, I'm sure it won't hurt!
(10/12/1990)

Spoken Words From My *Heart*

LOST

When we're together I feel a sense of trust
Just to see your beautiful smile, to feel a rush of lust
You make my skin crawl, make my heart throb
When we're not together all I do is sob
I really don't know where we went wrong
All I can remember is all the love was gone
I pray sometimes we could rejoice
I turn and look back and can only hear an imitation of your voice
I wish I could turn the clock back to when we fell in love
I'd worship it like you were a gift from above
Right now all I can do
Is sit and hope it will come true
The love was real
If only there was another chance to feel?
Please call and let me know
That our love will get another chance to re-connect and grow
I don't know how to say
Your love means so much to me in every way
Please tell me where you are
Out of touch, out of mind, you just seem so afar
Give me the straighten of how you feel
Tell me our love was not fake, at one time so real
Please just take me out of this maze
People tell me I'm just going through a simple phase
But if only I could find my way out this time
O promise you'll be the only love, forever on my mind.

(10/25/1990)

Dedra Haynes-Waller

What Happened?

Where did I go wrong, what did I say to hurt you
Like a burning in my heart, the feelings I have are so true
I can't remember what I said but you disappeared so fast
Was it I love you or will our love last?
I don't quite understand why you said you love me
I don't know why you began to stray away, that's something I couldn't see
Maybe you think I'm too young for you
Hey I can do whatever I want to
Tell me why didn't age matter when we first met
Our love began to grow, we were right on track
Tell me where I went wrong, was it something I said to hurt you
I was forever real, not fake believe me, I did love you
I know I can't change the way you feel
You never tried hard you just wanted to deal
This other person who's in your heart so steep
I don't envy her for it's me that you hurt so deep
I understand now better than I did before that I'm the one
All the times we shared we had way too much fun
There's one thing that you really must know
My feelings are strong, but I will let go
Take these words as a gift and not a threat
I respect your choice and believe me, I won't sweat
All I wanted was for us to have a relationship and just to be loved for me
I cannot be duplicated and that you will see
Trust in my word
Like none you've ever heard
I want you to be happy and not sad
You'll see I'm the best you ever had
So thank you for showing me the way
I just can't explain it; really I don't know what else to say
People called me stupid; some called me crazy, for talking to you again
Hey, it's life a game that's hard to win
So take it from me you're a hell of a man
One who thinks and believes he can do anything he can
Yet, I'll remember the rock; I'll never forget the sea
Just like you'll always remember the best times you had were spent with me!
(11/13/1990)

Spoken Words From My *Heart*

9

Dedra Haynes-Waller

Lord I Need Your Understanding

Lord, help me to understand the things I can't change
To accept the things and people who come and appear to me strange
I need Your help to carry on
I need a little help so I won't go wrong
Just a little guidance to help me see things through
More knowledge so I will know exactly what to do
My life had been shattered in to so many pieces, some I can't find
Every day I ask and pray that You'll help & give me peace of mind
Bad luck to anyone I just couldn't wish
But for those who would need food I pray for a blessed dish
I would never wish bad things to anyone -
like I have experienced in the past year
Only lots of love from the heart of someone close or very dear

Lord I know you can do anything at any hour
I believe in You and know there is no greater power
While I'm down on my knees
I beg you dear God to take care of me please
I've been told that You gave my son the biggest gift
that anyone could ever give
But I don't understand why You didn't let him live

So for now Lord I can only hope and pray
That I'll get to see him one day
For I know that I am still blessed
I still have a little girl walking around in her pretty little dress
Take care of me, for I don't want to keep asking why
So for now help me to raise my little girl, so I don't continue to cry

(2/1/1993)

Spoken Words From My Heart

Where am I and what do I do?

Sometimes things don't go the way we plan
Other things counter act different from what we understand
Life sometimes seem so unfair
Hard to realize too uncommon of a pair
The days go by and we're still in a daze
Wondering how long will we continue in this maze?
Maybe I'm in the wrong relationship you think to yourself
Maybe it's the wrong type of living I need to put up on a shelf
Meanwhile life's gradually going on to a place you don't even know
Places where no one would ever want to go
Think about it and make a decision and think of giving
Maybe I need a change of this horrible living
Then you'll see things aren't so bad
You'll find a person better than the one you had
Change is always good and helps a lot
Turning for the best is like hitting the jackpot

(2/5/1993)

Dedra Haynes-Waller

Forever In My Heart

C — Cares I feel deep down inside

U — Understanding I try to hide

R — Rules that we all have to follow

T — Trouble you missed without sorrow

R — Rivers you crossed along your heavenly way

E — Ease that heaven will display

L — Love I will have you forever

L — Laughter I will remember when we were together

RIP Mom...

Never take for granted when God has closed a door
Always try looking to the hills for there is a lot in store

Even when lonely or feeling blue
Remember a father's love is God's love and He bestowed it in you

Don't be so quick to give up, always try to forgive
Don't have too much pride, because our Father died so that we could live

(3/19/1993)

Spoken Words From My *Heart*

13

Dedra Haynes-Waller

Time is Ticking

It's been two months that my heart was washed away
Two months of heartaches, lost, gone to return some day
No one knows my pain, no one knows my sorrow
No one knows what today will bring or what happens on tomorrow
All we know is what goes on today
All we can remember are the things that went away
Lord I need someone to tell me everything will be all right
Blessed be to God all I need is to see my way to some light
Two months ago I lost my loving and dear son
Why dear God did this happen why didn't I get to keep this one?
One of the things I wanted in my life to love
You're keeping him with You in the gates of Heaven above
Lord why can't I shake this awful pain
What's going to happen to me, will I remain sane?
All I wanted was to have my daughter and my son
Somehow death stepped in and won
You tell me *it* didn't win, but still I don't know what to do
I lost my son, and I still have a lot of questions to You
Please God let this aching heart of mine heal
For time is ticking and it's hard for me to deal

(3/19/1993)

Spoken Words From My *Heart*

What's Going On?
How, What, When, & Where

How did you get here?
Where did you come from?
How did you get here?
How do you know you're welcome?

Sometimes people appear
And no one gives the invitation
Some people appear lost without
A reservation

You have to know your meaning
For being here
You need some type of clue
To why you'll stay there

Lost with no idea of where
Your going and where you'll stay
Leaves you in an undirected path
Somewhere lost every day

You need to find your way and
Find a place to go
Soon, someday so your life has
A meaning then you'll be
Happy and you'll know

Know what's going on
And how you got to this place
Then life won't seem so challenging
A struggling race

(1/19/1994)

Dedra Haynes-Waller

Here for the Changes

Did you ever think of what
Your purpose was here on earth
Did you ever think of the
Wonders of life's, birth
People are placed
In our lives for a reason
Some are only here awhile, lifetime
Some come every season
Our relatives are here to serve a purpose to us
To have as a part of our family tree
Some come in and out to teach us
Certain responsibility
People we love, come and go
Some stay near and some stay afar
Some people just come through our lives
Only once passing, like a moving car
We all are on this earth to serve
A purpose and good deeds for a reason
Wonder what you're here for and whose
Life you'll change this season
Here for the changes
Yes someday you'll see
Hope you change someone's life
For the good hope you can help someone
Like me

(7/10/2000)

Spoken Words From My *Heart*

There's Been a Change in My Life

Through all the laughs and all the cries
Through all the sweet hellos and the sad goodbyes
Something happened so fresh and so brand new
I found the love of Jesus and a special friend too
My life was changed so swift and it happened so fast
Everything that was around me explained my life, it was my past
I thank God for saving me, just when He did
All of my bad ways He's changing and bringing out the good that was hid
Yes I've had some more hard days and more of wondering too
But thanks to God I know where my help comes from to bring me through
Yes now I can tell someone in need of help that truly God is the way
I am a witness that He shelters me all along, every day
Now that my life is changed and I'm made brand new
I thank God for brighter days even when I'm feeling blue
Now I can say to my kids what's right from wrong and help them
In truth and not live a lie
I thank God for just giving me breath to want to live and not die
There's been a change in my life
Not only am I a child of God I will be a good wife
I want to be real and just be true as they come
To be a witness for Jesus, and remember where I come from
Yes time goes by and never to return
Thank God I know better now for it's always a lesson to learn

(10/1/2002)

Dedra Haynes-Waller

18

Spoken Words From My *Heart*

Is it a game or what?

Now that I realize that the time has past
I understand how the game of love goes, it goes so fast
At first I was unhappy and sort of confused
Now it's kind of clear, now I'm only wondering is it a game misused
Some people take love for granted and always for a game
But now as I get older I see you go in willing to tame

So when life's not treating you like you think it should
Just look up toward Heaven and just pray that it would
As life goes on you must seek God no matter what with all your beings
The longer you're in darkness the harder it is to find love and life's meanings
When you find God and learn to love someone in faith, truth and so real
God opens doors to feelings you never thought you could feel
Love is so beautiful and something magical
Kind of like a lovely rainbow so far out, so radical
Then it becomes a reality that love is not a game
You love unconditional and you're never ashamed
Remember life is important, not a game
Go in willing to love and not willing to tame.

(10/01/2002)

Dedra Haynes-Waller

Mothers Aren't So Bad

Becoming a mother you thought was easy
Just living the life letting go, feeling breezy
Once you realize that someday you'd grown up
The motherhood life didn't seem so easy, kind of felt caught up
Little loved ones so beautiful and innocent is all you can,
Remember that comes to mind.
The late nights, the early rising and all the hot temperatures,
All of which weren't so kind.
Oh what a gift of love God gave to you
But looking at your life you wonder now, what do I do
Becoming a mother you thought, yes I have a baby doll
You got ready to just run out, then a little voice you heard call
Baby-baby's on your hip and then by your side
Taking care of kids that's your job, you're a mother and you can't hide
Yes you've grown and so did the kids, things really aren't so bad
Wow, you tuned out okay, the best mother they had.

(8/8/2003)

Spoken Words From My *Heart*

New Life

Thank God for Jesus and all that He instills
The gifts, the blessings and all that life wills
True men and women of God all around
Teaching us how to be loving and kind without a frown
Just being in the presence of your sisters and brother of Christ
Eases the tension and stress of all other strife
Like little children passing something around that they knew was good
Trees planted by the rivers of life that rocked in a storm but always stood
Thank God for a new life that shines so bright among men
Turning like the wind over and over again
Blessed be the name of the Lord and that entirety He is and stands for
That He gave us another chance to live, once more.

(8/8/2003)

Dedra Haynes-Waller

MANTLE

You are the mantle that sits high on a shelf
So everyone can see
God put you there, I don't know why
So don't ask me
You are so special that's why you are placed
Up so high on the shelf to sit
Fiery darts will come and
Some will hit
But the key to it all is not to give up
Knock the darts off
And please don't quit
You're the beam of light people needs to see
I saw it in you, now take a look at me!

(8/31/2003)

You Make Me Smile

Joy, peace and happiness
Love, smiles and gladness
Looking deep into your eyes
Overwhelmed with a great surprise
Your smile, your laugh is one of a kind
The thoughts of you blowing in my mind

Walking down a path of lovely flowers
Playing in the dark, during afternoon showers
The joy of holding you in my arms
While listening to the sweet whispers of your sweet charms
Feeling the beat of your heart next to mine
Beat by beat the joys of a wonderful, love line

Never feeling love like this before
Reaching out for your hand as I walk through the door
You excite me with your warm embrace and your kiss
Like a fairytale you just don't want to miss
Overwhelmed with a great surprise
Thank you for being that special apple of my eyes
You make me smile...

(1/4/2004)

Dedra Haynes-Waller

ROSES

Peddles that twirl around until they form a shape
Life's winding moments of how much one can take
Colors are so many, bright, dark, some mixed in a special blend
Like being inside a room of all kinds of people and not one a next of kin
Some people describe a beautiful woman as a rose
Even though she's had hard times, a lot no one knows
Beauty comes from the inside and is very hard to hide
Once you encounter with it, you'll keep it close to your side
All the twists that these roses represent and stand for
Shows, when place on a bare table, when you walk through a door
Am I a rose you ask yourself the question
You've had bitter times yet you kept your flavor, what a blessing
Roses are what God placed on earth to make someone's day brighter
Conjunction with the rose, He made a woman to be a lover not a fighter
So next time someone gives you a rose
Keep in mind that you're highly favored and in your life the favor shows.

(2/24/2004)

Where am I now?

Walking inside a dark tunnel with no one or nowhere to go
You're walking and praying that someday you'll know
People wander around almost all their life
Never knowing how it feels to be a loving mother, brother, sister, or wife
Soon you're almost to the end of your way
Then realizing the light you saw was the change from your night to your day
You get halfway and thought you were all alone
But, thanks be to God He sent someone else along
You meet in the middle and encourage one another that you can make it
Now the tunnel doesn't seem so dark and you start to take it
Taking the past and putting it behind you and underneath your feet
Opening your eyes only realizing you were now at your break of defeat
The tunnel was only dark and long because you fail to get up and move at times
Until you met up with the right one who helped you keep a peace of mind
Sometimes starting over is really not so bad
Holding on to something that's not there will only make you sad
Over and over is something you think about, wondering is it the right move to make
But living without happiness is not good for the heart for it only allows it to break
So the next time you think you're in a tunnel and it's scary and dark
Try taking two steps back and remember how you got to that mark
Don't forget you'll still need to pray
So you'll be able to see your darkness turn from midnight to day.

(2/24/2004)

Dedra Haynes-Waller

We Are Who We Are

Ladies, ladies, young women and little girls that fill this room
Happy to see your smiling faces of joy and not of gloom
First to the little girls, we're glad you're here to listen to a word
Glad you came to see examples of all that you may have heard
Young women this goes to you too
So you won't forget that great woman that came before you
Women, yes ladies are what we should be, upright ladies claiming our victory
Not just sitting on a stump like knots on a log to see, but teaching our blessed history
Now don't get me wrong I know some of us are afraid to share our past
Until we share how we made it over all the pain still lingers, and last
I used to party and have lots of fun, that's what I thought
When I let Jesus in, I realized it was my soul He bought
Little, big, young or old we all have to walk down life's path one day
I came to encourage you to let Jesus led you, all the way
I was told I was precious even as a rose
The twist and turns that make up something so unique
Like our lives we're babies for a moment until we reach the next peak
Like roses, beauty comes from the inside and cannot be hid
Thank God He picked you to be His special kid...

(3/13/2004)

Closer or Not!

The closeness is so far from me now
Times have passed and a lot has changed without me knowing how
Trying to hold on and praying I don't lose my grip
Trying to keep moving forward asking God, not to let my feet slip
For so many nights I wondered how things changed like a blink of an eye
Then when the morning comes all the questions had answers and yet I still asked why
So close but yet I still can't catch a hold
So close but yet so far, I watched my life unfold
Not knowing which way to turn or how many country roads to take
I find myself asking God to help me, for I'm in a winding of give or take
Just a few more rivers to cross and a couple of valleys too
Keeps me praying for help, that I'll stay close to you
Soon someday this will all be clear and I'll see your plan
Then the times you've pushed me back, shows me you didn't need my hand
The closeness is so far from me which I desire to have again
The time has come when I know this is a fight I can't win
Please dear Lord, when I fall so close to the ground and no one can come to me
Give me the strength to know, it's you that I need to see
Trying to keep moving and stay on the right track
Dear heavenly Father, keep my front, sides and my back
For your forgiveness is what I long for and to have someday
The light beneath my darkness is forever, what I pray!

(4/26/2004)

Dedra Haynes-Waller

28

Two Knocks Out

Going around in the same circle, once again
What part of this lesson did I not understand?
Was it I forgot to stand, when you wanted me to just take a rest?
Did I forget that, I had to do what I could, and to try my best?
Sometimes I know I should have spoken up, when I just kept on the silence
Thinking that it would play a big part of keeping away the violence
But, dear Lord, that part I think I got
So why is this circle back to haunt me, or is it not
I questioned myself of the chapters that I've had to read
Some came back with unpleasant grades, others were good yes indeed
I tried not to think the chapter of love was the only one that was screwed up so bad
Then I looked at the chapter of forgetting and leaving it in the past
Those chapters I didn't quite understand the grades or the scores
But those were only read if you didn't pass those chapters you'll see it some more
One chapter said, "Who's going to knock you out"
Well, I thought I had that one under wraps but later
I didn't even know what it was all about!
Trying hard to master a book that has no meanings to all the words
Not even hearing the voice, only pieces was all I heard
After falling to my knees with nothing but hurt and despair
I started wondering how in the world, I even went there
Apart from my feelings and so far from the world
I began to ask myself am I still a little girl
Around and around you find a circling of dreams that never came true
Once again, another knock and it's a daze of not knowing what to do
Becoming a messenger of a book of hard knocks
Trying not to leave out any details making sure there's nothing I forgot
Then you learn to read with care and understanding, a lot seems to be clear
That's when you can help someone, who's close, far, or even near
To learn and do something about it is always a challenge that works
But to learn and remain the same doesn't change your life, it only hurts
So get off the road if you find yourself lost
Time and life's precious moments passed, is how you'll pay the cost!

(5/19/2005)

Spoken Words From My *Heart*

FATHERS

Fathers, to all that are in some way a father
And those of you who take out the time for other kids
Even when it could become a bother
With no added strain nor stress
Like helping your child get out of bed and
Helping them get dressed
Being a role model is something else that fathers do
By setting examples of their lifestyle from the old to the new
I know it's hard to say no, without breaking a sweat
But in order to teach, you have some goals that have to be met
It's okay to laugh, joke and play around
That shows a child life's not so mean, yet dad acts like a clown
Even when it's time to cry and you don't hide your face
Let's your child know you too, have some bad days but there's a better place
When you have time to show them how to be kind and polite
Just remember that's the child that you tuck in at night
For all of you that's so clean-cut and divenere
Little ones are watching you, even trying to smell the cologne you wear
When you're walking around smelling so fresh and so clean
Make sure your heart is right, and always say what you mean
As you're walking before your kids remember to watch as well as pray
That God will keep your paths straight, not to lead them astray
Someone had to show you the way
Remember you too, were a child one day
Hope these words have touched you and even your heart
For God places fathers here for children, right from the very start!

(6/16/2005)

Dedra Haynes-Waller

Tell Me How Many Times

Lying in bed without a care in the world
Am I only your play toy or your imagined girl?
You walk around with your chest poked so far out
With your head stuck up in the air really high
I wonder is this real love, or am I something to do
While you pass me by
Trying to keep a clear mind of everything, life has to offer ahead
It gets so hard knowing there's another, while you lie instead
So many unpleasant encounters when things are cool
And sweet dreams on the other hand yet, feeling like a fool
To understand life's ups and downs even the twists or turns
Must we travel the same road when you know it offers bruises and so many burns
Lord, help me to understand this test I must take
Is there a part I must learn from my own mistakes?
Trying to have a love that's just right or even just be true
Breaks my heart to know a man can't travel, unless he travels with two
I'm standing before you Lord to ask you for some help
This twirl is tearing me apart, each rip, I've felt
I often say to myself is it me or you
Do I make you so unhappy to do the things that you do
After a while you start to become numb, thinking this is how things will be
Then appears a wall, here comes the blinders now and you no longer can see
I pray to God that the sweetness and specialness of life will soon appear
I didn't come this far to let the devil take me back to a place of despair
Please Lord, hear my cry and understand my humble prayer
I'm trying to endure, for this is a lot for me to bear

(7/21/2005)

Spoken Words From My *Heart*

Today & Tomorrow

Today I lift my hands in surrendering motion
Today I ask for a glance of life's devotion
Tomorrow I'll ask that the skies remain blue
Then I'll ask if I'm worthy of you
The hills get higher a mountain turns and they narrow more than ever
The shadows so heavy, not knowing how to deal with the pain, but however
There is a name that I do know and believe
There are times other than death, when one's heart grieves
Torn so, til your no longer but in pieces, not halves, you are weaker than before
But shattered to the max until you're wondering how, just how much more
To stop and ask, what did I miss?
Becomes like a wildflower in a summer bliss
Not trying to cover your head or who you are
Is like holding up a blood stain banner in the desert afar
But, oh what do we know and who did we forget
The one and only Savior who could get us out of this pit
Today is another day my hands are up in the air
Today I know things will happen and the others we can't compare
Tomorrow I'll ask oh how much or how long will this journey last
Then I'll ask was this just a thing of my past
Dear God, this day I ask of Thee
To hold my life in Your hands and keep Your grace all around me
Today, today is all that I can pray
Please keep me dear Lord, for this is all I can say
(3/13/2006)

Dedra Haynes-Waller

Where's the truth?

There are some things people see that aren't always true
Then there are others that live to make your heart blue
Coming and going not knowing if you're at a point of no return
Feeling the tightness as your heart begins to burn
Looking into a woman's eyes who's been hurt on numerous times
Is like looking in a vacant house with half opened blinds.

You'll never really see what's really in it, nor get the true effect
Because things have been hidden to cover up what's inside not ready to be met
There are some things people see that are true
It's when they see the real you

Up and down, round and round
Without even making a sound
Once you get out the things you hid within
The real you shows up in your daily grin

Looking in a woman's eyes who's met God and feels reassured
It's like shaking hands with someone whose illness has been cured
Because a lot of things can be hidden and some are never even told
Try enjoying the reality of life, so your blessings will unfold.

(3/13/2006)

Am I worthy?

Once I regain my self-worth, of the cost my life represents
Once I reveal that the cost is priceless, how many will get these hints
Maybe too many are caught up and scared to face reality
But God showed me Him, in many of my technicalities
His blood was shed with the utmost price
He suffered for all of us, and yet we turn and think twice
Yes wondering if we should do right or how many times should we do wrong?
Then our lives end up being some old tired song

People take so very much for granted until their close to the end
It's like shattering a lifetime relationship of a close friend
Yes I know God sometimes chose to play a part where it's needed
But why don't the other person take what is in deeded
A drop over here and a big loss over there
How can people be so comfortable hurting others and not even care
The mistakes we make and time to this screeching cry
Only takes me back to what He did for all of us, and why

The cost is so priceless that we shall be reminded more than one day
How He took so much along the way
Lord please give this ol' child of yours another chance
I don't want to be left behind, because of a second glance
My self-worth I need restored today
I'll be the one who'll be on my way
I thank You for the mind to pray
Grateful to you for the price you had to pay!

(5/12/2006)

Dedra Haynes-Waller

Happy Birthday

I've searched hard and tried to find the right gift
But nothing comes to hand or to mind
I pondered over what would be the best, then I realized
I was running out of time so to my surprise I had it all along
God gave me a gift of encouraging words, and it wasn't in a song
Words of encouragement to let you know what you mean to me
I'm thankful for you are who God has called you to be
When things have been gloomy in my life
I remembered the words you spoke, without strife
Also the words that you carefully speak
Teaches me how to pray to be humble and meek
See there's a lot of things I can say to let you know
Just how special you are
Your presence alone, says you are one of earth's shining star
Keep being who you are, please don't second guess yourself
God gives you this wisdom and knowledge to use and not to be kept on the shelf
When you think sometimes if your light shines among men
Keep letting God lead you for He can be your only true friend.
So on your special day
Thank God you were able to see another wonderful birthday!

(5/11/2007)

Spoken Words From My *Heart*

What a Time, Shock, in Life

Days have passed and moments slipped away
Tears have been shed, yet still there comes another day
Wind blowing from north to south, dreams shattering east to west
Before and after comes along with this daily test
Words streaming all around in my mind
One after the other causing me to lose track of time
My days have passed and the months are flying by as words are hard to tell
Some things you get a chance to correct others seem to drift down a hollow well
Moments, seconds and brief thoughts of the steps of what to do next
Like traveling through a maze, the mind starts to become complex
How's there no room for me but so much room for you
Blinders cover the rainbow and the only color that seeps through, is blue
Is that a sign that I'm still in a ray of sunshine on the other side
Does that mean as long as I can see one color, I know I'm still on a good ride
How can the sun shine again through all this blue?
Can the colors of a brighter life, come to me too?
After the rain has passed and the clouds began to move back
How long does it take for good times to show up, just where I'm at?
You try all your life to do what's right and love others
Back to backs in a crowded room, leaves no space for good brothers
Unspoken words that just won't seem to go away
Causing my heart to skip, not knowing what to say
I'm told, that you'll be a better person, and to just hold on
How can you hold on to a love, which is strung along?
When the days passed and the moments run away
How can you tell the rope you're holding is in favor your way?
So as you take this daily test
Remember your colors or you'll create a mess
Some messes leave a lasting stain
Others take over with doubt, and leave no self-gain
So keep in mind the color was blue
Save room for other colors and they'll remember to save some for you

(6/29/2009)

Dedra Haynes-Waller

Running, trying not to leave what God has for me!

Blessings coming in many ways
Just before the blessings, why so many trial days
Yes they come to make you strong
Problem is they last… too long
Some trials have different tests at the end
You take one day at a time, sometimes having to start over again
Unseen and yet they're in your spirit to kind of prepare you for the ride
Some out of nowhere, how could they hide?
Blessings on the way for this you're very sure to see and smile
Conquering of the blockers, you walk on through every trial
Can this get any harder, why did you ask?
Now this has become a hurtle instead of a simple task
Oh, but still walking with much stride
Knowing that I can't have not an ounce of pride
Not in this situation, too much pride is not good
Knock down drag out, oh how I wish I could
Just for a moment to just blow them all away with just one wish
Doing the right thing in honor, step in the right direction, a road surely not to miss
Things travelling by a hundred miles per hour
Still you remain in control to sustain such power
Little did you know, God was there all along to hold your hand
Whispering in your ear, I told you… put no trust in man
Bless me now oh how my heart longs to be out of this mess
Being so hurt, yet to find you're in another test
Some blessings we receive because we do what's right and obey in the storm
Some we allow to go by unused, because we couldn't hold out, we became worn
Blessings follow the trials and most of the test
Once you come out, God shows you He's the very best
So stay strong and keep your place in line
For sooner or later this battle will have run its course, and also lost its time
Help me stop running,
for this speed sometimes makes things fall off without my knowledge
For I don't want to leave anything God has given me,
for this journey is like going to college
Being equipped is always the key
So I want to stay focused to receive just what God has for me
(9/10/2009)

Spoken Words From My *Heart*

There's a Shift Going On

You're slowly taking a precious gift
That God has given you
Why don't you have any value?
Of what lays before you

How can you allow a gift God gives to be sifted
From under you, and not see it go?
Have you been attacked with blinders?
Or do you even know

Slowly the feelings of trust, love
And even shelter that was once there
Starts to go away
Do you even care?

Trying to help the cause, as much without
Saying things are just really on the line
While praying for this
Is it just a waste of precious time?

If you have answers that could be shared
Do you know how?
Will you rather the road ends
Until the field needs a plow

Times ticking, God is moving
Will you be a part of the move?
Or will you stand still
And miss out or just lose

Move; move for there is a shift going on
For when it passes... remember it's gone!

(9/10/2009)

Dedra Haynes-Waller

38

Do you think I don't know you?

How can you chastise me for the decisions that I make
When I watch you turn love into a constant give or take
Do you really think you've pulled the wool so far over my eyes that I can't see?
Remember it was I that was with you in your lonely times, yeah me
When you move a certain way I know if it's for show or for real
When you speak, I know if it's sincere or you're underminded way of a deal
Do you possibly think I have no clue, just who you really are?
I'm walking with God, trust me He leads me by far
Your soft words and your ever so different swags
Do you realize that God's revealing everything, all the tricks in your bags
How could you think you're smarter than the Man above?
Yet you destroy what's precious to Him, He gave us His love
Walking by others day after day so empty, you are inside
You try and dress it up with your arrogance and little pride
I've watched you year after year portray to be this wonderful man
While all the time God was showing me if you can't stop him I can!
Trying not to blow your cover I sit back and someday hope you'll change
Now the more I look at you, things look rather strange
"Who are you?," is what I long to ask you from day to day
Sometimes wondering if you realize your sins you will pay!
With children in this world that belong to you
How in the name of God are you comfortable doing the things you do?
No no-one is to treat them without respect or dishonor
Yet you do that very thing to another, so where's your honor
Walking in dishonesty just about every day
No one can question you, because it's the bills you pay
Yap, yap to sounds of nothing is how I see your face
Hiding behind that black mask of lies and disgrace
Only God and time will change you and this is so very true
But remember who'll be standing by,
when you need someone to be there for you!
(9/20/2009)

Spoken Words From My *Heart*

Don't Let Your Life Lead You – You Might Want to Lead It!

Knock, knock and knock, hey my pride's trying to come in
Wait one second, my selfishness wont' allow me to bend
Hello, somebody, I have to get rid of some of this love
Because adultery just walked up and fornication too, is above
Man, what am I going to do now I just spotted greed and jealousy?
You know, I have to tuck what I can so no one will really notice that it's me
My body's firm and built up tight
What can I do with my bags of tricks tonight?
Maybe I'll get rid of a little honesty too, who needs that
Or maybe I'll hide a little trust under my pimp hat
The night is booming and it's fun and money everywhere
Shucks maybe I'll go another way, and hope the kids don't see me there
Turn my hat back and show off a little savvy-savvy, no one will think I'm married
Once I get what I want, I'll leave a little of what I carried
No one can see dogmatic ways is something that one can do
Should I have to suffer for it's my marriage number two
No way can't you see I got it going on, laid out crib, money and honey on the side
Look good when I want, share a little when I want,
so why can't I do a little seek & hide
By the way my mate's as good as can be
But, when the arguments come they only free me
Who? I have the plan, I do what I want, when I want, so how about that
Only sometimes it gets crazy when I forget and leave my hat
Big blow to the head and right hook to the body, I can't believe I'm going down
This hatred is no help; it can't get me off the ground
That was in my hat, man that's messed up
Reached for your wisdom and love; don't' have them neither I sold them for a buck
What about some kindness then, it might help; man I gave that to my other honey
All that bad and built-up stuff I had, now I'm down; where's my money?
No help, now you ask your family to come; did you forget you left them too
Knock down you're a mess, did you forget who was leading you
Oh no! It wasn't God; all you have to call for is a bunch of mess
Funny how things go around, because they all were a test
You failed with flying colors you didn't have a thing,
even lost those you tried to impress
You were led by the wrong things, pick it up and put it down
Now what do you have? No one's around!
So don't let your worldly life lead you, let God help you lead it!
So who's leading?
(9/20/2009)

Dedra Haynes-Waller

Dear God

I need you to help me stop this rage I feel on the inside
Sometimes it's overbearing till I just can't hide
I know I'm a good person, yet I'm under attacks all the time
Knowing that's the devil's job, God help me to recognize the signs
Being made strong in these times of weakness I know changes things
Yet the disturbance I feel in me, blocks my joy and my well-beings
I know you understand but you got to help me please
To fight back the devil and his amps of often times that he's a tease
Sometimes I feel oh God; I'm going to knock him out
Then I wonder or not who will win, or who has more clout
I know this may seem silly but it's how I feel
Trying and holding fast, why do I get these raw deals?
Not test, no testimony I know that's how it all works
Can a sister get a few weeks off, because this stuff really hurts
I'm asking you Lord for help,
to make my life just a little clearer for me to understand
These obstacles I'm enduring with this difficult man
Thank you God I know it's not all about him that's one thing I do know
I just need more guidance to choose wisely which path I should go
Please God this feeling inside is really not so good
I know You can help me; if nothing else,
please give me a sign to know that You would

(9/20/2009)

Spoken Words From My *Heart*

Do you really know?

Are you sure I'm in your circle of friends or likeness
Are you sure I'm in your circle, is this your act of kindness

If you knew me, why didn't you answer when I called?
If you knew me, how did you miss my hand and just let me fall
If you knew me, why didn't you lend me a hand when you saw I was in need?
If you knew me, how is it you couldn't hear my call for help or my cry or plead?
When you know someone you take time to know their favorite color;
Likes or even their favorite drink
You spend extra time helping them carefully make decisions and pray;
Pray and pray, while they think
You know their needs before they can even say a word
ou're tentative to their body language & their heart as it cries with words you've heard
You tell them thank you without feeling I had to do just that
You say you're welcome and bless you all the time no matter what or where you're at
You take the time to say everything's going to be all right
Even when you're not sure yourself
When you know someone; you forgive them and take all mistakes for love
And keep the good work stored upon a shelf
We must take notes and see what kind of person we really are
Should we be hiding behind reality or should we be like a shining star
So in your special time ask yourself do I really know you;
Or do you think you even know me

Start taking out the time to truly know someone else
So you can help them to be all they can be!

(11/6/2010)

Dedra Haynes-Waller

CHANGE

What can I say when the clouds start to shower over me and consume my thoughts
What can I say when my dreams seemed to have come to a sudden halt

How is it that when my wheels turn, I go nowhere?
Becoming so transparent to the sound of the still air
What must this time represent and how do I get past the point of nowhere

I am to be who God has made me to be
Will the day come, soon for me to see?
I am more than what my outside seems to show
I have greater values on the inside if you just took time to get to know

I believe my day of relief is coming sooner than I thought
I'm feeling a little better than what was sought
Believe me when I say I feel better and know that this is true
Because I can look at you and not feel sad or feel blue

Thank you for helping me realize I am someone special on this day
I will always remember you for the experiences you brought along my way
Change, change, yes change has come to stay
Thank you God for my change has come on this special day

(12/5/2010)

Color Tells It!

Red, green, yellow, bluer than the sky has ever been,
sharper than a two-edged sword
There You are appearing to me, my Lord
When this old day has come and gone and never to return
You'll be there for me to look, listen, and learn
Learn the ways of You and not of my own
Time passing so quickly, of to where I belong
Without a notice, first the moment, then a glance
When does the time come for me to enjoy and dance?
When is there a moment for peace?
A day of a gentle release
Making my way through this time seems like never before
Opening and closing I hear the doors slam once more
Yes, yes how does this train keep jumping off the track?
Is it something I'm missing or some spiritual attack?
Take me to a place of your grace and mercy,
to weather these great storms of mine
To Your place of peace and Your loving kind
Blue skies I pray to see
The sword You carry, thank You for protecting me
Yes I do believe there's also sunshine that will come
and the rain will go away
But I still need Your guidance to make it through this moment and this day
So as the days go and each moment gathers its time
Never take Your hands off of me, for I may lose my mind
Thank You God for each color tell its own story
For I'm interchangeable so that You'll get all the glory

(3/12/2012)

Dedra Haynes-Waller

HOME

Where do you call home, when there's nowhere to go?
Where do you call home, when you don't even know?
Where do you call home, when you don't know where you came from?
Nor where you belong or how to get to the right town
In the midst of people that are all around
Still feeling like you're all alone
Where do you go or where is home
Like being on another planet or out in space
Everyone looking at you, with looks of disgrace
Where do you call home when, there's no one to talk to
The feeling of so much emptiness because of being you
To even walk around with for days at a time so alone
Lord, oh Lord where is home for someone who has no place of their own
Lord, oh Lord when you feel like you don't belong
Please help me find out, where is home

(3/12/2012)

NON-SENSE

Blowing out hot air seems so comfortable for you
Making unknown sounds is a common thing you do

Not realizing your making noise with a tinkling sound
Too bad it adds up to nothing for it bounces, and just hits the ground

You speak as though you're so right and perfect towards men
If you could only realize your words should stay in a trash can

Canned up to not ever being heard for if spoken untrue
Remember unknown sounds and words make a fool of you

How can you not get what good you have in your midst?
How can your heart be so hardened to bypass the hurt, you dist

Someday you'll miss the jewel that you once had
Blowing out hot air will be your loss; yeah it will be too bad

Some people go a lifetime and never get it
Hoping you will someday change or quit

Hear the sounds of sweetness as it flows by
Then you'll see you needed to change and not, just I

(4/22/2012)

Dedra Haynes-Waller

Slowly Going Away

How can you not understand, I have so much love for you
When you do all the things that you do

Is it so hard to understand there is and can be true love
When you have an angel that was sent from Heaven above

Days pass not even knowing how many things you missed
All those special moments of love that gave perfect twists

No one ever knew how much nor how close you can come to the end
Until you realize you have lost a really close friend

So now your love that you had is slowly going away
Down into a pit, now you wish it would come back to stay

How much was the cost, you thought you had to pay
Why didn't you know it wasn't the time to squabble and play?

If you don't understand the love, you have is so dear
Once it's gone you'll someday wish it was near

Great lost that come from day to day
Hope you'll get it soon, because it's slowly going away

(4/22/2012)

If I...

If I told you that I loved you would you even care?
If I told you that I needed you would you be there

If I asked you for your love on a busy day
Would you take out the time to come by my way?

When the nights have taken their slow turn
Would you bring in the mornings with me, for my love to earn?

If I told you it was you that I truly miss
Would you stop by, just to give me your special kiss?

If I told you my heart was hurting and was about to break
Can you speak life to it that goes, straight to the ache?

After the workday has ended and you're not at my arms reach
Could you take out the time to hear of my day, through my heart's speech?

When you finally realize that I'm gone, for I needed you there
Will your heart ever show that you once did care?

For if I told you that I too wanted this to be
Yet you couldn't just take off the blinders to see, it was just me

(4/22/2012)

Dedra Haynes-Waller

How can you love and hate at the same time?

Smelling your scent from many yards away
Longing to see your smile come drifting my way
Your walk, your stern body, plays constantly through my mind
Yet your love is like a mucked stream, the bottom's hard to find,
Your touch brings joy and great sensation to one's soul
Yet your tongue speaks of things much too untold
Why does my heart spring a beat for your embrace?
The thoughts of deceit appears at a glance of your face
How can you love, truly love and hate at the same time
Why do you play mind games, like a drop of a dime?
When scars like these are created into someone's lifestyle
You become a victim, yes for quite awhile
Love and take
Then comes the misuse and the heartbreak
Along with the lies and the cheat
You then leave and create scars of deceit
Only wanting what's best for you
Causing someone to fall and not remember, left without a clue
Loving you so hard not realizing that it should be both ways
Complicated actions from you brings unpredictable days
Love and hate at the same time
Pretty hopeless and retracted bind
Retract your ways and maybe you'll receive different results that's for show
Unmoved actions will only lead you to another uneven flow
So with a little word of wisdom for the day
Remember love and hate has a thin line that may come your way
Special people require special love, and for sure one day you'll see
To love someone in return is truly the way love should be!

(2002)

It Comes Back!

Back in this place again with no one but God to turn to
Backed up against the wall making sure I know exactly what to do
My hands can't stop the words that flow in my heart
The more I write the more I realize how far we are apart
The lies always come around right back to me one way or another
Too bad you didn't know how to be a real man, or a strong brother
Allowing your sexual appeal to consume you this way
Failing to realize that someday you would pay

There's a place in a marriage you should never go
Especially to another woman's heart, not through her mid-night door
So as we go on living as nothing has happened from day to day
You'll see things are always off balanced in every way
Truth helps the heart to heal
Keeping secrets, soon you will have to face the ordeal
If only this could go away and not be true
Wondering how can I love this man, in you?

Trapping my mind in so many ways from time to time
Somethings make me wonder are you really mine
The day will come and all will be clear
You will be wishing you had me so close, and really so near
Don't underestimate the love that one can share
Just remember it's only so much that I can bear
We send things up in the air forgetting what goes up
Must come back down, when we sent out so much flack
Just know today, yes it will come back!

Dedra Haynes-Waller

UNIQUE

So unique from head to toes
Unique until your life glows
Don't get discouraged for who you are
You were placed on earth like a midnight star
Unique is what you are
God made us all different, some He made unique
If it wouldn't be for you this world wouldn't be complete
Always remember when to walk with your head
And toes pointed straight
For you'll be the one called on when
Everyone else is being fake!
So as you're adorned in how you dress in a room full
Of wild and crazy colors you will stand out so loud
Timing and knowing, you're the best thing walking
Always remember to, strut your stuff and make me proud
Proud to know that God made you just for Him
To keep this world on its toes
You will help them to sort difficult puzzles
When no one else really knows
So continue to help remind us how to analyze
What things are right before our face?
As God continues to give His mercy and share His unique grace!

Praying Hands

When you look at these praying hands
And wonder why God gave them to you
Thank Him for the instructions
And for giving you the book too

Just think of the lives you've touched
The hearts you made glad
And say wow, God made these old
Praying hands and they're not so bad

Not only were they made for touching
Holding or to just help keep warm
They represent the gifts that are within you
To heal, and help your magnificent charm

So when they begin to heat up and tingle
Know your gift is like none other
They come with a special jingle

They're open to help bring in new lives
And close to pray for the unseen eyes
So in the midst of praying for others
You know so well and love
Thank God for yourself for you're a
Wonderful gift that came from above

Dedra Haynes-Waller

Don't Give Up – Try Me & See!

Whenever God leads you from one place to another
Before wondering why, thank Him for your sister and brother
These times in your life you will endure so many different things
All of which elevates you to becoming a better human being
Take a look at what's going on all around you and how quickly
Those things do change
Some are so sweet and nice, while some others
Yet seem so strange

Knowing with God you can do and become anything
As long as you do your best
Don't count everything out when you
Fail one of life's tests

Remember to always pick-up and start over from where
You are, when you come across something that's difficult
Because God honors your willingness every time
You refuse to quit and especially when you don't give up!

(5/27/2012)

Spoken Words From My *Heart*

It is Well

Picking up and forgetting those things that had me bound
Kicking the trash out, not caring how it may be found
Yes, this is a new day and beginning for me
Green grass, blue skies, color yes color is all I see
Falling on my knees praying more and more brings much pleasure
Getting up knowing this struggle is worth all of my treasure

Never would have made it very far with all this luggage of mine
The weight has become so much lighter, now that I've left it behind
New start, new day is all my heart screams
Waking up knowing that God has delivered me and it's not in my dreams

So to you those walking in so much unforgiving in your life
It's not worth it to carry, for you will miss your blessing by holding on to strife
As I pick up the pieces of me, that were shattered all across the room
I feel a sense of joy and happiness that covered all my gloom
My days are brighter; my days are becoming so clear
Just to know your love, grace, mercy, and kindness is always right here

Thank you for loving me and holding me so close in your care
Keeps me striving to know you'll always be there
It is well with me, for I have longed for your touch
Yes! It is well for I know you love me so much!

(7/30/2012)

Dedra Haynes-Waller

God's Special Touch

For this time has come for me to say
That I'll see you again some day
Late on this past evening God came
I said yes I'm ready show me the way

My body had become so tired and weak
From fighting in this fleshly body so much
Please don't cry for I'm better now
God gave me His special touch

I know some of you are just as strong as me
So remember not to throw in the towel
For God will give you the strength you need
To win and not lose in defeat
For some things we can't win while others
We can beat!

I fought so long, for I love you all
So very much
But once again, I must say farewell
For I've accepted Gods' hand
With His special touch

Don't think for a moment this was easy
For me to say goodbye and let go
For I wanted to stay, but God knew
What was best, so I followed Him, you know!

Take the time that I've shared with you
To be a gift of all my love
That will help you get closer to God
So that I may see you again up above!

In loving memory, *Gail McJones*

(8/18/2012)

Spoken Words From My *Heart*

About the Author

Thanking God for where He has brought me up to this present time. I am a daughter, sister, friend, auntie, mother, wife, and grandmother. Most importantly, I am a child of the Almighty God! I have two children and a total of six children by marriage.

I love singing, my family time, and worshipping God. By God's grace, He has allowed me to record my first gospel demo titled, *Just Me, Dedra*. Songs include, *I Am What I Am, My Knees are Weak, and Thank You*. They were recorded at Demo-Ville Recording Studios in Titusville, FL, in April, June, and August of 2012.

I've been a nail technician since 1995 and I currently work at the Brevard Property Appraisers Office.

I am a member of the Love Center Church in Titusville, FL. I newly accepted the call of the Gift of Prophecy and received a certificate of completion June 23rd of 2012 from the School of Prophets under the leadership of Apostle Janet C. Moragne, Soaring Eagle Ministries, in Cocoa, FL.

With the help of the Lord, I'm always seeking what is ever in His will for my life. I say to all, trust in the Lord. If He did it for me, surely He can do the same for you!

Dedra Haynes-Waller

www.ingramcontent.com/pod-product-compliance
Lightning Source LLC
Chambersburg PA
CBHW060431050426
42449CB00009B/2236